Original title:
The Melody of Christmas Bells

Copyright © 2024 Creative Arts Management OÜ
All rights reserved.

Author: George Mercer
ISBN HARDBACK: 978-9916-94-086-0
ISBN PAPERBACK: 978-9916-94-087-7

Whispers of Winter Wonderland

Snowflakes swirl like dancers in the night,
The squirrels wear scarves, it's quite a sight.
Frosty noses and cheeks all aglow,
As snowmen chat about the winter show.

Penguins slide on icy slick trails,
While Santa debates which reindeer hails.
Elves play cards by the fire's dim light,
Gifting giggles with all their might.

Chiming Echoes of Yuletide

The cat in the tree makes quite a scene,
While cookies giggle, 'We're fit for a queen!'
Rudolph sneezes, the sleigh shakes in fright,
As stockings try to dodge the candlelight.

Wrapping paper has a mind of its own,
In the chaos, we laugh and have grown.
Mom's hot cocoa is a bubbly delight,
While the gingerbread men cheer for a bite!

Harmonies Beneath Frosty Skies

Icicles hang like tiny old chimes,
While snowmen sing about silly rhymes.
The dog steals a mitten, runs with a bark,
In this merry land, we glow in the dark.

Carols echo through the frosty air,
With voices that tickle, not a care.
Laughter dances like lights on a tree,
Tickling our spirits, just let it be!

Jingle Dreams in Silver Light

The fairy lights wink like stars in a fight,
While reindeer giggle at each other's flight.
Candy canes battle for a place on the shelf,
Holiday cheer is just being itself.

Frosty hats fly like frisbees of fun,
As children scream, 'Can we go for a run?'
Even the snowmen join in the race,
In this jolly game, we find our place.

Celestial Carols in the Silent Night

A jolly Santa lost his way,
With reindeer dancing, oh what play!
Elves in a sleigh, on sugar highs,
Singing loud beneath the skies.

Mistletoe hung in a crooked line,
While grandma's cookies disappeared just fine.
Laughter echoes, an upbeat tune,
As snowmen jiggle under the moon.

Frosty hats fly off his head,
While carolers sing, but then they fled.
One tripped on ice, what a sight!
And all of us laughed till we turned bright.

So raise a glass of fizzy cheer,
For all the blunders that we hold dear.
In winter's warmth, let joy unfold,
With tales of Christmas that never gets old.

Voiced Wishes in Silver Bells

There's something silly in the air,
As gifts get wrapped with utmost care.
Dad's lost the tape, and oh, that roll!
Buried in boxes, he can't find a soul.

Sister's singing with all her might,
Tone-deaf tunes that bring pure delight.
Mom shakes her head as we join the fun,
Laughing and snacking till the day is done.

If bells could giggle, they'd surely chime,
As Uncle Joe dances, stepping in time.
The cat's in a box, wanting to play,
While Grandma smiles, as kids shout hooray!

So here we are with wishes bright,
In silver bells ringing through the night.
With laughter glowing, hearts intertwined,
Making memories, one of a kind.

Dancing Notes of Winter Light

A penguin slipped on icy ground,
With flailing flippers, he spun around.
Snowflakes giggled, twirling about,
As laughter erupted, we all scream out.

Hot cocoa spills on dad's nice shirt,
While mime-snowballs fly from sis with a flirt.
Chasing each other, round and round,
Winter's absurdity knows no bound.

We build a snowman with a strange hat,
One eye on a button, the other, a cat.
He tips over, but we don't care,
We applaud his fall with festive flare.

So let's dance under the starry glow,
With winter silliness in full flow.
Here's to the laughter that we create,
In this joyous time, oh, isn't it great?

Chimes of Joyful Tidings

Bells are ringing, yet someone snores,
While cookies vanish behind closed doors.
Socks on the mantle, oh what a sight,
Hiding the gifts, oh what a plight!

A reindeer sneezes, then takes a bow,
While children giggle, "Oh, wow, wow!"
The cat on the tree is high-fiving stars,
As laughter erupts from beneath candy bars.

Uncle Bob's jokes, they never land,
But still we chuckle, it's all so grand.
Sparkling lights in a tangled mess,
Yet somehow, it's better, I must confess.

With gift wrap battles and tinsel fights,
Our quirks unite on these festive nights.
So let's ring out joy with each passing chime,
In this funny chaos, our hearts still rhyme.

Buoyant Notes on a Frosty Breeze

Jingle jangle goes the cheer,
Snowflakes dancing, oh so near.
Santa's sleigh makes quite a fuss,
Oh look! That's Uncle Gus!

Frosty sings, his buttons sway,
While reindeer munch on hay.
Hot cocoa spilled on Grandma's lap,
That's how we wrap up this trap!

Elves are giggling, what a sight,
Swinging bells, oh what delight!
Chasing mittens in the snow,
Oops! Slipped on ice, oh no, oh no!

Tinsel fights on the tree's top,
Snowman tips, oh what a flop!
With joy and laughter, we will roll,
A festive night that warms the soul!

Singing Stars Above a Peaceful Night

Twinkling lights, they wink and play,
Santa's got his dance today.
Rudolph rhymes with silly tunes,
While munching on those candy moons.

Chimney smoke, oh what a scent,
Laughing 'bout where the presents went.
Socks that stretch, a little tight,
A battle cry for love and light.

Gifts that giggle when they're shook,
What's inside? A funny book!
Carols mixed with silly sounds,
Happily lost in joyous rounds.

Stars are laughing at our fun,
Spreading love for everyone.
In this calm and cozy night,
Let's sing out with pure delight!

Frosted Chords and Warm Embraces

Frosty air and cozy hugs,
Mom's baked cookies, oh what cugs!
Dancing folks all round the fire,
Spinning tales that never tire.

Tickled toes and silly hats,
Forgetful Santa, where's that cat?
Sledding down with those who squeal,
Laughter echoes, steal the wheel!

Ticking clocks and flapping wings,
Tinsel caught in all the strings.
Snowball fights with squeaky shoes,
Winter fun, we just can't lose!

Joyous voices, hearty cheer,
Merry moments, love is here.
Let the frosty chords unite,
With warm embraces, oh what sights!

Glimmering Sounds of Togetherness

Jingle bells on silly hats,
Grandpa sings with kitties and rats.
Together we play, oh what a show,
Laughter bursting just like snow!

Wrapping paper takes a dive,
Puppies frolic, oh, alive!
Squeaky toys under the tree,
Chasing tails is pure glee!

Noisy giggles, hugs galore,
Mom's in the fray, drops the floor.
Silly games with all the crew,
A merry band, a joyful zoo!

As bells ring out over the head,
Let love and laughter be widespread.
In every heart, a spark will stay,
Together we laugh; hooray, hooray!

A Tapestry of Sound and Light

Jingle hats on all the cats,
Dancing wildly, chasing rats.
Bells are jingling, what a show,
Santa's sleigh has lost its tow.

Elves are giggling, lost their way,
In the snow, they love to play.
Sledding down from roof to ground,
Chasing presents all around.

Frosted Melodies on the Breeze

Frosty noses, tickled ears,
Tangled lights bring lots of cheers.
Singing carols, all out tune,
Howling like a crazy loon.

Cookies baking, warm and bright,
Charlie's taking one, what a sight!
Spilling milk, now what a mess,
Santa's list is quite the stress!

Bells Ringing in a New Dawn

Morning light, what a surprise,
Ringing bells will mesmerize.
Rooster crows, he's out of tune,
Hoping for a quick cartoon.

Snowmen dance with arms out wide,
Chasing dogs, they take a ride.
Laughter echoes through the air,
Hiccuping from frosty flair.

Symphony of Echoing Cheer

Reindeer pranced on top of sleighs,
Dizzy spins through snowy ways.
Laughing loudly, giving chase,
Falling down, they lose the race.

Muffins flying, what a thrill,
Husband's baking, needs a skill.
Decorations fall and crash,
Surprise party, what a splash!

Small Bells Sing Big Dreams

Tiny bells jingle, what a cheer,
Singing loud for all to hear.
Santa's sleigh on the rooftop glides,
Reindeer giggle as laughter rides.

Stockings filled with socks and snacks,
Elves are plotting sneaky hacks.
Chasing snowflakes, slipping fast,
Wishing this fun would forever last.

Cookies crumble, icing spills,
Merry chaos, lots of thrills.
Grandma's knitting turns to yarn fight,
In this madness, all feels right.

Under the tree, a cat pounces,
Knocking down gifts as it prances.
With each clatter and playful sound,
Joyful moments are always found.

Songs Wrapped in Flurries

Snowflakes dance through windows wide,
As sleds bounce down the snowy slide.
Voices rise, a chorus loud,
Singing silly, we're quite proud.

Frosty jumps with a wobbly jig,
While kids all call him a big twig.
Carrots nose and scarf askew,
In our hearts, warmth breaks through.

Hot cocoa sips, a marshmallow dive,
As everyone fights to stay alive.
Who can balance cups on heads?
We all giggle, slip, and tread.

With mittens lost and noses red,
Off on journeys, we soon tread.
Chilly giggles fill the air,
Every moment, joy we share.

Resonance of Evergreen Wishes

Tinsel glimmers, shining bright,
Our Christmas tree, quite a sight.
Broken ornaments spun like tales,
As laughter fills, the spirit sails.

Dancing gingerbread, sugar high,
Filling dreams that touch the sky.
With every bite, a silly grin,
Who knew cookies could make us spin?

Presents wrapped, but who's to guess,
That inside lies a big ol' mess?
Ribbons tangled, chaos swirls,
In our hearts, a dance unfurls.

With every jingle, we've a blast,
Mem'ries made, they surely last.
So grab a friend and join the fun,
In this whirlwind, we've just begun.

Chiming Through the Ages

Bells are ringing, what a sound,
Making laughter all around.
Time to gather, friends and kin,
With each chime, our hearts do spin.

Old folks share tales with a grin,
About reindeer games and snowball win.
Silly hats atop our heads,
In this madness, all dread sheds.

Games of charades and dancing feet,
Merry chaos, oh so sweet.
Who can do the best chicken dance?
Every failure brings a chance.

Through the seasons, memories blend,
With each story, love we send.
As these bells ring louder still,
Our hearts sway to a happy thrill.

Echoes Through Frosty Nights

Snowmen dance with twinkling lights,
As penguins slide on frozen nights.
The squirrels wear their winter hats,
And join the fun with jolly chats.

Chimneys puff with candy cane,
While reindeer play a silly game.
Frosty giggles, jolly cheer,
In every home, the laughs draw near.

Hot cocoa spills on frosty toes,
As snowflakes tickle little nose.
The cat plays chase with twinkling threads,
While sleepyheads snore in their beds.

Echoes of laughter fill the air,
With crazy socks they all can wear.
In frosty nights of silvery light,
Every moment feels so bright.

Bells That Sing of Hope

Bells are ringing, silly things,
Dancing ducks in bright red wings.
The snowflakes play a quirky tune,
While bear cubs bounce beneath the moon.

Penguins wear their best bow ties,
Sipping cocoa under frosty skies.
As friends assemble for the feast,
The laughter grows, it's not the least.

The elves are mixing up some stew,
With sprinkles, giggles, and doughnuts too.
With every bite, a cheer we make,
As holiday bells start to shake.

Bells that jingle, bells that shine,
With every clang, joy intertwines.
In moments shared, with laughter life's hope,
We find the ways together to cope.

Harmonies in a Silent Night

A cat on the roof sings a high note,
While kiddos dream of a candy boat.
Santa's sleigh gets stuck in a tree,
With reindeer laughing as wild as can be.

An opera of giggles fills the town,
As snowmen wobble and fall down.
The moon chuckles, sweet and bright,
In silly dances of frosty delight.

The stars hum tunes of fun and cheer,
As penguins gather for the show, oh dear!
With popcorn flying and drinks that spill,
Laughter echoes up the hill.

Harmonies of joy fill the night sky,
With wishes floating and spirits high.
Together we share this quirky scene,
In every heart, a festive dream.

Jingle Dreams and Snowflakes

Dreams of raisins on the roof,
As gnomes are dancing, what's the proof?
Snowflakes land on noses bright,
A giggling pup steals starlit light.

The cookies hide and play a game,
While goofy smiles come to acclaim.
Carrots vanish, no one knows,
What happened to those little toes?

In a flurry of gifts and wraps,
Jingle dreams are filled with laughs.
Each tangled ribbon tells a tale,
Of merry mischief in snowy trails.

With every jingle, joy unfolds,
In cozy stories, new and old.
We celebrate with a wink and a swirl,
Jingle dreams in a wondrous world.

Harmonized Wishes on Winter's Breath

In the frosty air, a sound rings,
Penguins in hats dance and sing.
Hot cocoa spills with a little cheer,
Laughter erupts as snowflakes appear.

Socks on the roof? What a sight!
Cats in boots, ready to fight.
Snowmen sneezing, what a blast!
With each jingle, a giggle is cast.

Reindeer are juggling, much to our glee,
Grannies are racing down the old tree.
Bells are ringing, in stylish tunes,
As birds wear scarves, and tap-dance soon.

So raise a glass of fizzy delight,
To wishes and whispers on this cool night.
With every jingle, we play the game,
In the winter's breath, we're all the same.

A Ringing Call to Celebrate

Bells are clanging, what a show,
Mother's fruitcake flies, away it goes!
Dancing llamas, join the fun,
Santa's stuck up there, oh what a run!

Elves are breakdancing, oh what a sight,
Chips and dip, a festive bite.
Gingerbread men on roller skates,
In snowball fights, they're sealing fates.

With cheer we gather, friends near and far,
Sipping hot cider from a jam jar.
As the bells chime, we all will huddle,
Sharing smiles, and candy-scented cuddles.

So let's toss confetti, make it rain,
With joy overwhelming, forget the mundane.
In the chaos of jingles, our hearts take flight,
A comedic symphony, bask in the light!

Bringing Joy in a Chiming Wave

Ringing sounds from rooftops high,
Santa doing flips – oh me, oh my!
Cookies that dance, and pies that sing,
Sprinkled with giggles that laughter brings.

Socks piled high, a fetching sight,
On the cat's head, they're snug and tight.
Jingle bells and giggles blend,
As kiddos chase, around the bend.

Snowflakes tumble, and snowmen grin,
While penguins skate, all set to win.
Mugs overflowing with marshmallows and cheer,
In this wacky wonder, we gather near.

So gather 'round the jolly table,
With tales and snacks, oh so stable.
With each clink and clang, we light up the night,
In the warmth of each chuckle, everything's bright.

Snow-Sweetened Symphonies

Oh what a sound, the snowflakes hum,
While Frosty's tipping a can of gum!
Pigs in scarves run down the lane,
Jolly laughter, a wacky refrain.

Lights are twinkling, like fireflies,
As grandma's reindeer start to rise.
With cocoa wars and silly games,
The night's alive with giggling names.

Singing squirrels join the fun parade,
With tiny drums, the beat is laid.
Caroling frogs in top hats sway,
While the clock chimes in a quirky way.

So let's toast marshmallows, big and small,
As jolly jesters entertain us all.
With chimes and chuckles, we end the fest,
In the spirit of joy, we are truly blessed.

Chiming Hearts Across the Snow

In winter's coat, we skied so fast,
The snowman winked; we flew right past.
With jingle hats that dance and sway,
We laughed aloud, come join our play!

Hot cocoa spills, a marshmallow fight,
Our mittens clash, a flutter of white.
The neighbors sigh, their windows closed,
While snowballs fly, we're never dozed!

Around the tree, we twirled so bright,
Our furry friends in hats take flight.
Every cheer rings out with glee,
Oh what fun, just you and me!

As bells ring clear, we shout hooray,
For doggy shenanigans lead the way.
With laughter loud, we'll dance and sing,
What joy a silly winter brings!

Songs of Peace Beneath the Stars

Under the sky where laughter soars,
We gather 'round with fuzzy chairs.
The stars they wink, the moon's in tow,
As giggles bounce like frosty snow.

A cat in boots dances with flair,
A goose joins in, we cannot bear.
With sleepy eyes, the night unfolds,
As tales of missed socks start to hold.

Jingle bells dented, what a sight,
Two cousins chase with sheer delight.
The quiet moments turn to jest,
When pillow fights are half the quest!

So here's to us, all bundled tight,
With dreams of donuts filling the night.
In joyous harmony, we'll cheer,
For fun and friends, we hold so dear!

Lullabies for a Winter's Night

In socks that slide upon the floor,
We dance and laugh, we want some more!
The cookies call from 'round the way,
We munch and crunch, oh what a day!

The clock ticks slow, it's time for bed,
But sneaky snacks pop in our heads.
With giggles soft, we munch on treats,
Our pillow fights are now complete!

Muffins land like fluffy clouds,
While Santa's sleigh speeds past the crowds.
We dream of snowflakes, pure and bright,
And tickle fights beneath starlight!

So let us drift through dreamland's door,
With giggles that could fill a store.
For winter nights craft joy anew,
In silly dreams, just me and you!

Festive Echoes in the Air

Amidst the trees, the squirrels prance,
In reindeer hats, they break their stance.
With treats galore, they scamper high,
And giggles burst as snowflakes fly.

Our hats are crooked, scarves askew,
As snowmen tumble; oh what a view!
With carrots lost, they still stand tall,
They wave their arms and start to call.

In cookie dough, we slip and slide,
While tasty treats we cannot hide.
The laughter rings, a joyful tune,
As sprinkles land beneath the moon!

So grab a friend, let's dance and sing,
In every heart, the joy we bring.
Echoes of laughter fill the night,
With frosty fun, oh what a sight!

Frosted Nights and Candlelight Songs

Snowflakes dance like silly twirls,
Lights are winking, laughter swirls.
Santa tripped on his own boots,
Elves are giggling in their suits.

Fires crackle, marshmallows roast,
A cat stole Santa's midnight toast.
Reindeer zoom with silly grace,
One lost a bag and fell on space.

Carolers sing with off-key cheer,
Their notes make everyone want to steer.
Mittens tangled in a big heap,
While grandma snorts, she's fast asleep.

So raise a glass, let's toast the night,
To funny sights and pure delight.
Around the tree, we dance and sway,
Making merry in a humorous way.

Voices of Tradition and Cheer

Hats are worn, but sideways, too,
A dog just stole the whole fondue.
Grandpa's socks are red with green,
A sight that's hard to keep unseen.

Mistletoe hangs but no one dares,
To kiss the cat, she's caught unawares.
Bells are ringing, but so off beat,
As cousins argue who's got the best seat.

Cookies crumble, the milk runs dry,
Little Timmy's wearing a pie.
Tradition calls, as laughter flows,
In this sweet chaos, joy only grows.

So grab your hat and spin around,
For funny stories will abound.
In this festive hustle and delight,
We find our cheer, by firelight.

Whispers of Silver-Gilded Dreams

Dreams of snowmen, with big round heads,
Whispering secrets, scaring the beds.
Kids in pajamas, with faces so bright,
Sneaking cookies in the dead of night.

Sprinkles of sugar on every treat,
An army of ants will soon take a seat.
The cat in the tree is quite aloof,
Chasing stars that dance on the roof.

Jingle bells rattle like a runner's race,
As grandma spins, she lost her place.
Sleigh rides happen beneath the moon,
While someone hums an offbeat tune.

Here's to the night of silver dreams,
Where laughter flows in endless streams.
These playful moments, we treasure well,
In simple joys, we find our swell.

Melodies Adrift on the Snow

Songs of winter float and fade,
As snowflakes perform a silly parade.
A penguin slid right into my door,
While all the kids yelled, "More and more!"

Chorus of children, voices collide,
As they take turns on the sledding ride.
Frosted cheeks and hot cocoa spills,
While dad attempts to try all the thrills.

Frosty's nose is a bright red ball,
And nobody knows how he'll not fall.
Gifts wrapped tightly with tape and bows,
As Uncle Fred tries on the new hose.

So gather 'round, let's laugh tonight,
With silly tales and hearts so light.
A melody here, a giggle there,
In the warmth of joy, together we share.

Serenade of Snowflakes Falling

Snowflakes dance like tiny clowns,
Dressing rooftops in soft gowns.
Sleds fly past like letters tossed,
With giggles echoing, never lost.

Snowmen wobble, carrots skewed,
They look more like a veggie brood.
Their button eyes, a cheeky glint,
That says, "We're chubby, not a hint!"

Hot cocoa spills, a marshmallow fight,
Whipped cream smiles, oh what a sight!
Snowball armies, fierce and bright,
Laughter fills the snowy night.

Carols in the Crisp Evening Air

Chorus of cats jingle and meow,
As singers hit notes no one can allow.
A dog joins in, with howls so bold,
Clearly thinks he's got the gold.

Neighbors peek from windows wide,
To see who sings with furry pride.
Off-key moments bring such cheer,
Encore giggles fill the atmosphere!

Join the dance with slip and slide,
Each move a funny mishap ride.
Laughter rings where carols play,
It's the best kind of holiday.

A Symphony of Festive Lights

Twinkling bulbs, a dizzy sight,
Some are crooked, but that's all right.
The cat yanks strings, like a pro,
Leaving us caught in its twinkly glow.

Neighbors boast their lights ablaze,
While squirrels plot in a zany craze.
Who can outshine? Who's the spark?
A light fight soon will leave its mark!

Inevitably, someone trips a wire,
And suddenly, there goes the fire!
Laughter erupts in pure delight,
As we fix the chaos brought to light.

Twilight Tunes of the Holiday Spirit

Evenings filled with pots and pans,
As everyone stirs their funny plans.
Burnt cookies smoke, a fragrant treat,
With giggles mixed in with the heat.

Teenagers groan at leftover tasks,
While Auntie rushes, shouting "Masks!"
The mischief brews as parents sing,
But it's kids who pull the real bling.

Yet as the night grows fun and bright,
We toast with mugs, feeling quite right.
Laughter twirls like sparkling stars,
In this festive place of quirky jars.

Celebratory Chimes at Day's End

Bells are ringing, what a sight,
Everyone's dancing with delight.
Elves in stripes just missed the beat,
Tripping over tiny feet.

Gingerbread men on roofs do roam,
Stealing cookies, making home.
Santa's sleigh is quite a mess,
Where's the reindeer? Take a guess!

Hot cocoa spills in happy cheer,
Splashing friends who gather near.
Tinsel tamers hang with flair,
One got stuck, now he won't care!

Joyful laughter fills the air,
Like a cat stuck in a chair.
As the sun sets, what a show,
Chimes await the night's soft glow.

Lifetimes of Wishes in Silver Tones

Wishes flutter, shine like stars,
Kittens chase 'round candy cars.
Jingle all the way, they say,
But here the cats just want to play.

Pine trees wobble, ribbons fly,
Ornaments that wave goodbye.
A garland made for a big gal,
Turns into an elaborate pal.

Santa's list was quite a feat,
He miscounted each sweet treat.
Naughty schools of fish and frogs,
Dance beneath the Christmas logs.

So here's to laughter, hugs, and fun,
Under the moon, our hearts will run.
Life's a gift, with silly quirks,
In merry tune and joyful smirks.

A Symphony of Hope in the Snow

Snowflakes dance like tiny bugs,
Winter coats and snugly hugs.
A penguin slides, a snowman grins,
While holiday cheer just begins.

Hopscotch on a quilt of white,
Snowball fights from morn till night.
Friendly faces start to glow,
One fell down, now moves in slow-mo!

Muffins popping, ovens bright,
Whiskers bearded with some white.
Singing loudly off-key tunes,
Our laughter links with winter moons.

So join the dance, don't lose your toes,
Each giggle spreads, just like your nose.
A symphony of joy, no dread,
As snuggly blankets warm the bed.

Echoes of Laughter in the Air

Jingle hats upon our heads,
We dance like turkeys, full of bread.
With every hop, a giggle's found,
As snowflakes twirl, we spin around.

Uncle Joe misplaced his shoe,
We search the trees, who knew it too?
With candy canes, we poke and prod,
Our laughter echoes, a joyful nod.

The pets all seem to join the fun,
Chasing lights, they dash and run.
A game of catch with a paper ball,
The sounds of joy, we hear them call.

So grab your mittens, let's invite,
The neighbors for some holiday fright.
With cocoa spilled and marshmallows here,
We toast to laughter and festive cheer!

The Soundtrack of Winter's Heart

Bells are ringing, what a sight,
As we trip on tinsel, pure delight.
A snowman grins, with a goofy hat,
While dancing squirrels make us laugh at that.

In every room, a bear in socks,
With silly faces, it's quite the frocks.
The cat jumps high, a real ballet,
Side-stepping puddles—oh, what a play!

Eggnog spill from Auntie Sue,
Painting the floor in an amber hue.
We slip and slide like it's a race,
In our living room, what a wild place!

The music plays with joyful chime,
Funny moments that last a lifetime.
With laughter ringing bright and clear,
Our hearts will dance through every cheer.

Chants of Hope and Togetherness

Gather 'round for tales untold,
Of frogs in scarves and birds so bold.
Each story spun, a humorous plight,
Turns a cold night into pure delight.

A turkey prank gone terribly wrong,
Flapping wings and a catchy song.
With sprigs of mistletoe overhead,
We smile at chaos, no tears to shed.

Frantic cookies made by dad,
A sprinkle of joy, oh that's not bad!
With every bite, a chuckle's shared,
As icing drips, our stomachs bared.

So lift a glass of fizzy cheer,
To moments made when friends are near.
In every giggle, let love be found,
In our little world, happiness abounds!

Celestial Notes of Peace

Stars above with twinkling eyes,
As we toast marshmallows to the skies.
With laughter shared by fireside glow,
We sing off-key with a merry show.

A mitten lost down by the stream,
In the frosty air, a wild dream.
We race through flurries, not a care,
Dressed like snowmen, with puffs to spare.

The jingle bells play a silly tune,
While we enjoy a pie made by the moon.
With goofy hats and crazy shoes,
We dance away every holiday blues.

So let's make merry, our hearts in flight,
As giggles spark through the chilly night.
In the warmth of love, we cheer and sing,
For joy and laughter are the best of things!

Celebrating in Tinkling Harmony

Dinging and donging, the bells take flight,
Jingle on rooftops, what a sight!
Santa's stuck, oh what a mess,
Elves giggle loudly, you must confess.

Charming tunes fill the frosty air,
Frankie the reindeer, does a funny glare.
Mittens and scarves, all mismatched styles,
Laughing so hard, bringing the smiles.

Glimmers of Light and Sound

Twinkling lights dance on the tree,
Wobbling ornaments, oh don't you see?
Grandpa's snoring? What a loud boom!
While cookies vanish, it's Santa's room!

Snowmen wobble, hats way too big,
Chasing the dog, it's quite the gig.
With laughter and joy, we're all aglow,
Gifts in the corners, a bright tableau.

Tones of Togetherness and Warmth

Gather around for the feast tonight,
Auntie spills punch, oh what a sight!
Cousins are tossing marshmallows high,
While dad's stuck under the table, oh my!

Silly old songs fill the air with cheer,
Tickling the toes of those we hold dear.
Kittens chase ribbons, the dog steals the pie,
In this silly chaos, we all laugh and cry.

Annual Refrain of Kindness

Squeaky horns and a trumpet's grace,
Neighbors complain, finding their space.
Cookies exchanged with a wink and a smile,
Giggling at stories that last quite a while.

Funny old sweaters, we wear with pride,
Sneaking some candy, oh what a ride!
Under the mistletoe, a cheeky kiss,
Memories made in the holiday bliss.

A Tapestry of Twilight and Joy

In winter's chill, the snowflakes twirl,
A squirrel in a scarf begins to whirl.
Hot cocoa spills on all grandma's shoes,
As we laugh and chime with holiday blues.

Jingle bells ring, but oh, they are late,
The cat has claimed them, it's now her fate.
With reindeer games, oh what a sight,
They're stacking presents, all piled up tight.

Gingerbread men run for their dear lives,
While frosting fights on innocent pies.
Our tree leans left, a little too much,
But the glow it brings? Oh, such a touch!

Wrap me in tinsel, oh don't you dare,
I look just like a sparkly bear!
In twinkling lights our laughter befalls,
A tapestry spun from glittering thralls.

Dancing Shadows in Joyful Revelry

In the kitchen, pots start to sway,
As grandma's recipe goes way astray.
The turkey's dancing, what a grand sight,
While Uncle Joe plays the flute in mid-flight.

Mittens lost in mysterious ways,
Swipe that cookie—where'd that cat play?
The wreath on the door has a mind of its own,
It twirls and jigs like it's overgrown!

Snowmen arguing, who has the best hat?
The reindeers complain, 'Why are we fat?'
Elves throwing snowballs from rooftops high,
While laughter echoes as chuckles can fly.

With shadows that dance in the glow of the night,
We join the parade, oh what pure delight!
Sleighs filled with giggles and sprightly cheer,
In this joyful revelry, we hold dear.

Soft Echoes of a Love Renewed

Under mistletoe, we play peek-a-boo,
While sipping our cocoa, like lovebirds do.
Grandpa's stories of shoes made of meat,
Are met with a chuckle, oh what a treat!

A snowflake lands atop the dog's ear,
He shakes it off, giving us all cheer.
While laughter rings louder than bells in the morn,
A funny twist keeps our hearts reborn.

As carolers sing with such off-pitched glee,
We'll join in, harmonize, just you and me.
With cookie fights and flour on noses,
In this hallowed love, everyone dozes.

So let's toast to the quirks that we share,
With twinkling lights reflected in your hair.
In every soft echo, love's not untrue,
We find joy in laughter, our hearts are renewed.

Frost-kissed Harmonies of the Heart

Frost-kissed rooftops and chimneys that puff,
A snowball fight has everyone tough!
The dog takes a leap, adds to the fun,
While I'm left dodging—where's my hot bun?

Gifts come wrapped in a paper surprise,
With cousins who plot, oh what a disguise!
We giggle and holler, what mischief at play,
While great-grandma's vase slides swiftly away!

Elves take a stroll, all decked out in cheer,
While squirrels look on, their eye full of beer.
The sleigh broke down; the reindeer complain,
But laughter erupts like a holiday train.

So let's sing together, both jolly and bright,
With jokes and with pranks to anchor the night.
In this frost-kissed moment our hearts do align,
Creating sweet harmonies, fun and divine.

Echoing Lights of Christmas Past

Jingle bells in the night,
Clanging loudly, what a fright!
Cats jump high, dogs do a spin,
As grandpa dances with a grin.

Ornaments hang like fruits on trees,
Unruly kids climb with such ease.
The sweet smell of cookies so grand,
But who ate the dough, was it Aunt Jan?

Mistletoe hung, it's a scary place,
Uncle Bob has a smirk on his face.
Santa's caught with crumbs galore,
He didn't just leave; he's back for more!

The lights blink crazily, they thrill,
As the neighbors give all their goodwill.
One last cheer, here comes the feast,
Grandma's turkey: is it a beast?

Twinkling Tidings of Goodwill

Snowflakes dance and often twirl,
As puppies chase them, oh what a swirl!
Hot cocoa spills on socks and toes,
A perfect scene for silly woes.

Tinsel caught in Santa's beard,
Now he's looking a bit weird!
Comet and Cupid, racing bikes,
They zoom past, think they're new pikes.

Stockings filled with socks and hats,
Expecting treats, but getting rats!
These surprises bring endless cheer,
Who planned the pranks? You brought beer!

Gifts piled high, a funny sight,
Wrapping paper - oh what a plight!
Uncle Leo's sock, for Auntie Sue,
What a gift, just her size too!

Notes Cradled in the Winter's Embrace

The wind sings tunes through trees so bare,
All the critters stop and stare.
They gather 'round, both big and small,
For Christmas cheer in the snowy hall.

Snowmen dance, their hats askew,
While carolers sing, not quite true.
The dog steals a scarf, gives it a whirl,
As the toddler slips, in a joyful twirl.

Pine tree farts, or so it seems,
With a crackling fire and wild dreams.
Hot pies cooling on window sills,
Mom just called for no more spills!

Sweet pie fights in the kitchen flow,
Grandpa's grin as he makes dough.
A final chime, the clock strikes eight,
More giggles rumble as we all await.

A Celebration Born in Sound

Bells a-jingling, oh such fun,
Little ones racing, on the run.
Grandma's singing her off-key song,
We all hum along, can't be wrong!

Candles flicker, shadows play,
Mice get loose and join the fray.
Oh watch the cat, she's on a prowl,
A Christmas heist, with a cheeky growl.

Laughter echoes, filling the hall,
As cousin Tim takes a mighty fall.
The punch bowl spills, splashing all around,
It's a festive circus, with joy profound.

Frosted gingerbread, sweet and tough,
Giggling kids can't get enough.
As jolly times come to an end,
Thanks for the mess, it's all a blend!

Achorus of Laughter and Light

Jingle all the way with glee,
Santa tripped, oh what a spree!
Elves in a tangle, what a sight,
Ho, ho, ho, it's pure delight!

Cookies gone, who took the stash?
Rudolph's nose lit up like a flash!
Mistletoe hung, oh awkward kiss,
We laugh so hard, it's pure bliss!

Snowballs fly and hats go askew,
Chasing each other, joy breaks through!
Winter wonderland, friends unite,
With giggles that bloom like stars so bright!

Tinsel tangled in grandma's hair,
We can't help but stop and stare!
In this crazy festive spree,
Laughter rings in harmony!

Blissful Serenades Underneath the Stars

Stars above are winking bright,
Singing tunes into the night.
A cat dances on the roof,
"Meow-mas" shouts from a goof!

Snowflakes crunch beneath our feet,
As we slide and then we meet.
Who wore socks with sandals out?
The laughter echoes all about!

Hot cocoa spills, oh what a mess!
Sprinkles fly—oh, I confess!
Sipping with a silly grin,
We toast to chaos and we win!

Underneath this merry sky,
We share a laugh, a wink, a sigh.
With joy that twinkles from afar,
Our blissful night is like a star!

Joyful Refrains in a Starry Night

Under the stars, we gather near,
Singing songs, spreading cheer.
Snowflakes fall, we grab a hat,
What's this lump? Oh wait, it's a cat!

Sledding down the hill, oh so fast,
Oops, there goes our lunch—what a blast!
Laughter echoes through the air,
A winter wonder, without a care!

With carols sung in silly tones,
Mismatched socks and worn-out phones.
Grandma dances like she's spry,
Who knew she could really fly!

Gather 'round, hear the joyful hum,
As we roll on snow, here we come!
Giggling under the moon's bright light,
Our joyful refrains bring pure delight!

Glowing Notes of a Hopeful Tomorrow

The fire crackles with a cheer,
While Auntie dances, drink in rear.
"Look out!" we shout, but it's too late,
Her wig flies off—a funny fate!

Chests of gifts, but where's my toy?
Found it! Stuck in dad's old ploy.
He wrapped a lamp, what a surprise,
A shining beacon that never lies!

As we sip on fizzy drinks,
Little ones giggle, love it stinks!
Wishing on a star so small,
May laughter echo through it all!

In every heart, a twinkling spark,
Together, we'll dance until it's dark.
These glowing notes, a sweet refrain,
Bringing hope like gentle rain!

Serenade of the Season's Spirit

In a hat that's way too tall,
A snowman sneezes, gives a call.
Jingle bells on cat's new collar,
Dog runs off, oh what a holler!

Gifts wrapped tight with sticky tape,
Mom's mistaken fruitcake for a grape.
Uncle Joe's got mistletoe,
Kissing the tree, it's quite the show!

Carols Whispered by the Wind

The squirrel steals the candy canes,
While grandpa sings off-key refrains.
A reindeer flips, lands on a sleigh,
And giggles echo, "Not today!"

The frosty breeze gives cheeks a glow,
Snowflakes dance like they're in a show.
A choir of penguins sing with glee,
They're hoping for a nice fish spree!

Sweet Tones of Yuletide Cheer

The turkey's strutting for the feast,\nWhile kids plot pranks, oh what a beast!
A pie fights back with whipped cream flair,
And dad slips soft, he's unaware!

Lights are tangled up on the tree,
A puppy barks, "Just let me be!"
Grandma's knitting, but knits a sock,
"Uh-oh!" she gasps, it's quite a shock!

Rhythms of a Frost-Kissed Eve

The chimney sweeps with a loud thud,
Santa's stuck, what a big dud!
He wiggles and giggles, shakes with zest,
"Next year, I'll diet, it's for the best!"

The children toss snowballs that fly,
One hits the grill, oh my, oh my!
With laughter ringing, it's quite the scene,
Winter's antics make spirits keen!

Season's Greetings in Harmonious Chords

Jingle in the morning, oh what a sight,
Santa stuck in the chimney, oh what a fright!
Elves in a giggle, with cookies so sweet,
Frosty's dance moves are quite hard to beat.

Carols sung loudly, off-key and wild,
Reindeer are laughing, oh look at that child!
Gifts wrapped in chaos, a ribbon gone mad,
Mom's wearing a tree, isn't she rad?

Socks filled with candy, such flavors surreal,
A gingerbread house that's a little too real.
Hot cocoa spills over, marshmallows in flight,
The cat's on a mission to find the lights bright.

Wrapping paper battles, a paper cut's doom,
The tree is still standing, but where's the vacuum?
Season's greetings echo, with laughter in tow,
The funniest moments are what make it glow.

Whimsical Waves of Holiday Cheer

Dancing with snowflakes, a whirl and a spin,
Uncle Joe's in the kitchen with flour on his chin!
Gingerbread men running, oh look at them dash,
While Grandma just wonders where all her cash!

Sledding down hills, we navigate with ease,
But all of a sudden, we find ourselves knee-deep in cheese!
Mittens mismatched, a fashion faux pas,
Chasing the dog, who has run off with the straw.

Penguins on ice skates, taking a slide,
Mom's holiday sweater is quite a wild ride!
Snowballs a-flying, a battle so fun,
Unexpectedly hitting the neighbor's old son!

Laughter erupts with each festive cheer,
As doorbells ring in, spreading good cheer.
With cookies and cocoa, and snacks all around,
Oh how these whimsical waves do abound!

Rhythmic Chimes in Candlelit Rooms

Singing with gusto, the rhythm in play,
The cat's on the table, oh whiskers, away!
Bells on the tree sway, a mystical tune,
While grandpa tells stories of a strange balloon.

Mistletoe hanging, the awkwardness grows,
Cousin Bob's sneezing, inside one of those!
Pies in a frenzy, oh what a delight,
A chaotic feast, oh what a night!

Candles are flickering, shadows that dance,
Sister's new haircut, not quite by chance.
Chiming and laughing, tuna on toast,
While dad wears a sweater that he loves the most.

Laughter echoes through every room,
As holiday spirits start to bloom!
Rhythmic chimes ringing with glee,
In these candlelit rooms, we just let it be.

Enchanted Tones Beneath the Mistletoe

Silly hats donned, we gather around,
Dad's trying to be funny, but he is just loud!
Lights twinkle brightly, but one's gone rogue,
A dance in the kitchen with marshmallow vogue.

Grandma's good cookies? A recipe tease,
They're more like rocks, oh dear, say cheese!
Singing in circles, off-tune yet so strong,
The spirit of laughter where we all belong.

Snowmen are wobbling, with eyes made of coal,
As cousin Timmy goes chasing a roll!
Kissing under leaves that are green and strange,
Silly traditions, they never do change.

As night gently falls, and stories unfold,
We sit by the fire while the fun is retold.
Enchanted tones blend our hearts into cheer,
In this festive season, with all we hold dear.

Resounding Joy Across the Square

Jingle hats and wobbly feet,
Santa slipped on his own sweet treat.
Elves are dancing, making a fuss,
As reindeer roll in the snow, oh what a bust!

Frosty neighbors share their cheer,
But watch out! Here comes a rogue reindeer.
With a wink and a wink, they crash the feast,
Fueled by cookies, they laugh like beasts!

Laughter rings and the kids all squeal,
One runs off with a snowman's meal.
Hot cocoa spills as friends all race,
A merry muster on the chilly base!

So if you hear a chuckle tonight,
It's just the bells bringing sheer delight.
With goofy moments ringing so bright,
Join the fun and dance 'til the moonlight!

Each Note a Glistening Memory

A squirrel stole my shiny bell,
He gave it a toss, oh what the hell!
Now he rings it loud with glee,
Dashing round like he's fancy-free!

Mom's baking cookies, can't find the flour,
The cat's in the mix, oh what a power!
What a clatter with every whisk,
They'll taste like magic, or just a risk!

Dad in the corner, wearing a grin,
Had too many sweets, now he can't spin.
He twirls like a tree, all arms and legs,
While Auntie chuckles, she points and begs!

Each note we hum bursts with cheer,
Memories ringing, we hold them dear.
With laughter echoing, we "ting" and "tonk",
Creating magic in the fun-filled thunk!

Joyful Voices in the Frost

Outside the snowflakes start their dance,
But first, we must give Frosty a chance.
A carrot nose flops, oh what a sight,
As he waves 'hello' with sheer delight!

Snowball fights ignite the rowdy crowd,
With giggles and shouts, they cheer out loud.
A toss and a flutter, who'll get hit next?
Then down goes Tommy, oh, he's perplexed!

We sing a tune, voices all blend,
While trying our best, we twist and bend.
Forget the words, we just hum and clap,
Our chorus of chaos is the best mishap!

Laughter will guide us 'neath starlit skies,
In every frosty breath, friendship lies.
So join the fun, let your spirit lift,
With joyful voices, we share this gift!

A Dance of Ringing Wishes

The bells are ringing, the kids have come,
With mismatched socks, oh what a sum!
They twirl and spin, they bound like frogs,
While parents chuckle at their silly logs!

Each clink and clatter gets tangled tight,
As gifts go flying across the bright light.
One box opens with a mighty roar,
And out hops a puppy, oh what a score!

With wagging tails and floppy ears,
He steals the show, spreading all the cheers.
A dance of wishes floats around,
With laughter and barks, joy is unbound!

So let the bells echo loud tonight,
In every heart, we set things right.
With wishes ringing, let's join this dance,
Laughing together, let's take a chance!

Threads of Light Through the Frost

Jingles jangle, oh what a sight,
Noses red and boots too tight.
Tinsel tangled in my hair,
Santa's stuck! Oh, do beware!

Icicles hanging like old cheese,
Squirrels darting with such ease.
Gifts are wrapped but cats won't stop,
Chasing ribbons while I drop!

Snowflakes fall like fluffy bread,
Mittens lost, oh, where's my head?
On the porch, a snowman grins,
Waving high as laughter spins!

Twinkling lights all through the night,
Elves on break, but what a fright!
Oops! A bump, the tree goes crash,
Jolly times, in festive bash!

Singing Together in Silent Moments

Whispers blend with laughter loud,
Ticklish feet beneath the crowd.
Carols sung, oh what a mess,
Socks on heads? Truly, I guess!

Hot cocoa spills on grandma's shoe,
Oops, that wasn't meant to do!
Cookies vanish; who will claim,
The sneaky cousin, such a shame!

Jolly dances in the hall,
Uncle Fred, he spins, he falls!
Silent night, ho ho ho,
As the dog steals the mistletoe!

Everyone grins, it's festive cheer,
What a sight, we laugh, we cheer!
With each note, the smiles swell,
Giggling under the holiday spell!

Refrains Carried on the Wind

Chimes are ringing, who is near?
Fido's barking, sounds so clear.
Fridge is empty, where's the pie?
Did it vanish? Oh my, oh my!

Snowmen wobble, hats askew,
Why does Frosty look so blue?
A carrot nose just rolled away,
Let's have fun, it's time to play!

Mittens flying, hearts collide,
Laughing kids all full of pride.
With each note, the joy expands,
Bouncing snowballs from our hands!

Through the laughter, tunes arise,
As we dance beneath the skies.
A silly song from every heart,
In this season, play our part!

Frost-Kissed Carols of the Heart

Bells are ringing, duck in flight,
A rooster sings, is it the night?
Mistletoe hangs, but wait, oh dear,
Caught the cat, not Santa, here!

Laughter echoes 'round the tree,
While Dad trips, it's hard to see.
A dance-off starts, who will jive?
It's chaos, but we feel alive!

Snowball fights and hot tea brew,
Marshmallows melting, it's true blue.
Grandma's sweater, colors bright,
Twinkling eyes, what a silly sight!

As we gather, love's the theme,
In this whirlwind, we all beam.
Harmony floats, a sweet embrace,
Merry moments in this space!

Lanterns of Sound Amidst the Ice

Bells are ringing, ice is slipping,
Sleds are flying, laughter's dripping.
Snowmen dance with carrots bright,
While kids wear socks that don't quite fit!

Candles flicker, shadows play,
As snowflakes join the wild ballet.
Reindeer prance, they trip and slide,
With candy canes, they take a ride.

Hot cocoa spills, the mug is tipped,
The dog is chasing, the cat has flipped.
Giggles rise, the snowball flies,
In this winter fun, no one cries!

Cheers ring out, the night is grand,
Funny hats stuck to each hand.
In the sparkle of the snow so bright,
Our laughter echoes through the night.

Winter's Chorus of Laughter

Snowflakes tickle, noses freeze,
Frosty air, a giggle tease.
Jingle hats on heads they sway,
As everyone comes out to play.

Tinsel wigs and silly frowns,
Bouncing through the snowy towns.
Bundled up in layers thick,
A snowball fight turns into a trick!

Chubby cheeks and frosty toes,
Slip on ice, oh how it goes!
Reindeer trot with comical flair,
In this joyous winter air.

Choruses rise, all voices blend,
Silly songs and laughter send.
Mirth is found in every place,
As smiles brighten every face.

Songs from Distant Lands

An elf with socks, oh what a sight,
He jingles and jangles, what a delight!
From lands afar, the tinsel flows,
While a penguin spins on his toes.

Frosty dances in a tutu neat,
Snowflakes join in on frozen feet.
With reindeer games and laughter loud,
They form a frosty, funny crowd.

Candy canes and gumdrops bright,
Introduce a new dance tonight.
Silly hats and jolly tunes,
Make way for snowball-hurling goons!

Songs are sung from coast to coast,
In the chill, we laugh the most.
Sharing joys from far and near,
Winter's cheer, we hold so dear.

Chime of Love and Giving

Bells are ringing, laughter flies,
Tickled toes and goofy sighs.
Gifts wrapped up in paper bright,
With bows that wiggle, what a sight!

Warm hugs shared and cookies passed,
The joy of giving, unsurpassed.
Funny sweaters on display,
With reindeer noses going 'Hey!'

Silly stories fill the air,
As friends and family show they care.
In this season of joy and cheer,
We laugh aloud, the end is near!

So raise a toast, let laughter flow,
In this season, love will grow.
With chimes of joy, our spirits lift,
As we share upon this gift!

Shimmering Echoes of Love

In the sky so bright and clear,
A jolly snowman sings with cheer.
He dances round on feet of ice,
While penguins giggle, oh so nice!

The stockings hang, so full of glee,
With candy canes from A to Z.
A cat slips in, its paws all white,
And starts a snowball, what a sight!

The laughter rings throughout the night,
As reindeer prance, oh what a sight!
They play tag with the moonlit stars,
While elves ride by in shiny cars!

A hot cocoa spill makes quite a mess,
But holiday joy is always the best.
With cookies dancing on the floor,
Who knew that treats could have such lore?

Chimes Marking Time in December

The clock strikes joy with silly chimes,
As Santa squeals in silly rhymes.
His sleigh gets stuck in some fresh snow,
While laughing kids from rooftops go!

The gingerbread man runs oh so fast,
Chasing squirrels—what a blast!
With frosting eyes and a gumdrop hat,
He turns to dance with an napping cat!

Mistletoe hangs, oh what a scene,
As Uncle Bob tries to be keen.
He slips and slides on the icy floor,
And ends up heading out the door!

Bright lights twinkle with diamond hue,
As snowflakes join the jolly crew.
Each carol sung turns into a jest,
This merry season truly is the best!

Whispers of Frost and Family

The frosty air brings giggles wide,
As Grandma's quilt is thrown with pride.
She tells tall tales by the fireside,
While grandpa sneezes, what a ride!

The kids sneak bites of pie and cake,
While roaring laughter starts to break.
A snowball flies, a poppy blast,
And Uncle Fred gets hit—oh, that's fast!

In cozy corners, stories blend,
Each sweet moment, we defend.
With silly hats and warm delight,
Our hearts are full, our smiles bright!

Together around the festive cheer,
Laughter rings, oh how sincere.
With family close, it's just the best,
These frosty whispers never rest!

Journeys in Notes of Kindness

A sleigh ride through the snowy mist,
Where jingle bells lead the way they twist.
The laughter echoes, a merry tune,
While frosty critters dance by the moon!

The elves are busy, oh what fun,
As they bake cookies for everyone.
With sugar sprinkles and giggles sweet,
They make a feast with joyful feet!

In every corner, kindness flows,
With secret gifts by frosty bows.
And with each note, we raise a cheer,
For love is found when friends are near!

So join the song, let laughter soar,
In every home, heart, and door.
For in this journey, we all shall see,
The spirit of joy is meant to be!

Milton Keynes UK
Ingram Content Group UK Ltd.
UKHW021843151124
451262UK00014B/1284